Indiana's Own

STORIES FROM THE HEART WITH RAY RICE

Indiana's Own

STORIES FROM THE HEART WITH RAY RICE

INDIANA HISTORICAL SOCIETY PRESS • WISH-TV, CHANNEL 8
INDIANAPOLIS 2003

Printed in Canada by Friesens Corporation.

The paper in this publication meets the minimum requirements of American National Standard
for Information Sciences—Permanence of Paper for Printed Library Materials, ANSI Z39.48-1984.

Library of Congress Cataloging-in-Publication Data

Rice, Ray.
    Indiana's Own : stories from the heart / with Ray Rice
        p. cm.
    Fifty stories based on a television program anchored by Ray Rice.
    ISBN 0-87195-169-X
        1. Indiana—Social life and customs—Anecdotes. 2. Indiana—Biography—Anecdotes.
    I. Title.

F526.6.R53 2003
977.2'043'0922—dc21

                                                            2003056585

Book Design by Patricia Prather, Dean Johnson Design

Dedicated to the good people of Indiana

Preface

As you browse through these pages, you will find fifty of the more than three thousand human-interest stories I was privileged to produce for WISH-TV in Indianapolis between August 1989 and July 2002.

This book is the result of thirteen years of traveling around the state and discovering some wonderful people and their stories. This was, however, not my discovery alone. Most of the story ideas came from someone else—a viewer, a friend, a colleague, somebody met in a chance encounter, or even a public relations person who thought to pass along a good story to me.

There was a time in my career when telling a hard-news story was my top priority. Over time, however, it became apparent to me that my place was among inspirational stories. Even today I can remember any number of times when I was so personally touched by what was shared with me and the camera that I was certain the Lord had given me a wonderful gift—the opportunity to find the very best in people.

With some exceptions, when time allowed, I produced, in the rush of deadline, one story a day, then moved on to do another. After looking back on them all, I have selected fifty of "Indiana's Own," not because these are my favorites or those that I consider my best work, but because I believe the people in them are worth another showing in a format different from the ephemeral world of broadcast journalism.

Fame and fortune as an author is not something that I seek. My purpose in bringing to print some of my stories on "Indiana's Own" is so that those whom I met will be remembered long past their brief appearance on television. My hope is that down the road someone will pick up this little book and see what fine and interesting people we have around us.

Many people had a hand in seeing the book through to publication through their work in editing, marketing, and design. At the Indiana Historical Society Press special thanks are due to Thomas A. Mason, Paula J. Corpuz, and Ray E. Boomhower for their work on the manuscript. My appreciation is also due to the marketing and public relations department staff at the IHS, including Brenda Myers, Catherine Bennett, Rachael Vaught, and Carrie Wood. Patricia Prather at Dean Johnson Design is responsible for the book's outstanding design.

Gratitude is also due to the staff and management at WISH-TV, Channel 8, especially Scott Blumenthal, the station's president and general manager. Without WISH's support this project would not have been possible.

Letter from the President

For fifty years now, WISH-TV has been covering history as it happens, reporting the news through both good times and bad—sharing stories about the people we call Hoosiers and the place we call home.

During twenty of those years Ray Rice served as NEWS 8's special assignment reporter and later wrote and produced thousands of stories in his daily segment, "Indiana's Own." Ray has treated television viewers to a unique look at the people and places all across Indiana. In *Indiana's Own: Stories from the Heart,* WISH-TV, Ray Rice, and the Indiana Historical Society are proud to share these stories with you.

We hope that you enjoy them.

Scott Blumenthal
President and General Manager
WISH-TV

Good Neighbor

Herman Beem   September 1989

Take a look around and you'll find some places in town that are not very attractive. Some people just don't seem to care about their neighborhoods.

Well, take a look at the median divider on Emerson Avenue between Sixteenth and Nineteenth Streets. It's not kept this way by any city employee or contractor. It's kept clean by Herman Beem.

Cars speed past and honk their hellos every morning while Herman cleans up litter. "I used to mow out in front here and it looked so darn nice," he says. "So it just gradually expanded. And, nobody told me not to. I was just thinking about how I felt about the median. I felt it should be clean and well groomed. That's the reason why I did it."

Herman gives us all reason to think. "Pretty buildings don't make a pretty city," he tells me. "It's the people. If you don't improve the quality of the people, you're not going to improve the city."

You'll find Herman out here in all kinds of weather. When I last saw him, it was in freezing rain. Yet, there he was, picking up after us.

Herman Beem retired from Eli Lilly in 1971 after twenty-five years with the firm's security department. Within a year he was picking up trash along the street where he lived.

RAY'S UPDATE: Mayor William Hudnut once presented Herman with a reflective vest, and he received one of several Community Service Awards from the City of Indianapolis. We also acknowledged his work twice on television. Herman continued his one-man cleanup campaign as long as he could. He died on January 3, 2000, at the age of ninety-three.

Friends

It's harvest time on the Mike Whicker place, but Mike isn't here this year. He was killed a few weeks ago when he fell off a silo on his property.

Farming, however, is a family affair, and in a broader sense all farmers are related. On this day they came to help bring in the harvest.

There was neighbor and friend John Hardin Jr. Ken Edmondson came, too. Don Cope was on his International Harvester. Allen Hardin. Rex Parson drove his Gleaner's combine five miles just to get here. Then there were the trucks. Don Goode brought his rig over and so did Bob Pedigo.

"Wasn't long after Mike's death that I started getting calls at my office from farmers and customers of mine that wanted to help out," says Jim Loughmiller. "And this is one way they could help out."

Loughmiller coordinated the harvest on Mike's one hundred acres of soybeans, and his Midland Coop donated the fuel. Everybody gave something.

"All these fellas that are here. They've got families of their own and crops of their

7

own to harvest," Cope says. "I know that speaking for the family that there's just no way that thanks is enough for what they've done here today."

Mike's brother John explains: "It's really incredible because of the help we've had here this afternoon. It sort of renews your faith in mankind. So many of the news reports you hear are negative about people, and this shows there are a lot of caring people in this world."

Mike Whicker sowed a good crop. About forty bushels per acre, they say. But, he sowed something else. Everyone said the same thing: if it had been someone else in trouble Mike would have been the first to help.

"Oh, yea. Definitely. That's the way Mike was," adds his nephew Tim. "He'd have been right behind anybody else, backing them up and helping everybody."

Tim agreed that the place won't be the same: "Not in the least bit. There'll be a lot of changes and nobody really knows what's going to happen yet. So, it'll be different."

Yes. It'll be different. This farm has been in the family for fifty years. Mike ran it with a youthful touch for the past fifteen years.

Mike Whicker lived to be only thirty-seven. But a man's life is measured in more than years. It is how he sows his crop that determines the quality of his harvest.

RAY'S UPDATE: The Whicker farm met the same fate as many family farms, being sold in 1990. Mike's wife Liz moved into town, remarried, and reports that Mike's four children are doing well. In 1997 Mike's nephews, Tim and Doug, began dairy farming again. People still tell Liz that they miss Mike's smile, laugh, and jokes.

Message from Oz

Cheryl Ann Silich   November 1989

There are times when you know you are not in Indiana anymore. Walking into Cheryl Ann Silich's apartment is one of those times.

On the walls, tables, the mantle—everywhere—there are reminders of a wonderful fable, *The Wizard of Oz*. Cheryl's guests are just like Dorothy when she woke up in Munchkinland.

"They're just in awe. Their eyes widen and their mouths drop," Cheryl explains. "Other people almost stand back from it and they're kind of sizing up the room like a little Munchkin is going to come running around from the corner or something."

Remember? There's the Scarecrow without a brain, the Tin Man without a heart, and the Cowardly Lion with no courage. With Dorothy by their side, they go down the Yellow Brick Road merrily singing, "We're off to see the Wizard, the wonderful Wizard of Oz."

Like the rest of us, Cheryl has seen the movie more than once. But she has decided to live in Oz. She dusts her collection while listening to the movie soundtrack. Her telephone answering machine asks the caller to leave a number or, as the voice of the Wicked Witch of the West threatens, "I'll get you my pretty. And your little dog, too!"

"Ding Dong the witch is dead. The Wicked Witch. The Wicked Witch. Ding Dong the Wicked Witch is dead."

Beyond the dreams and fun and the fantasy though is a deeper meaning in this fifty-year-old movie. There is a message for everyone.

"Somewhere over the Rainbow bluebirds fly. . . ."

"I like the over the rainbow theme to the movie," said Cheryl. "And to my life, that you can just keep working and keep achieving and keep trying to make a difference in the world."

"And, what is over the rainbow for you?" I wondered.

"For me? Hopefully, helping to find a cure for CF."

Cheryl is executive director of the Cystic Fibrosis Foundation of Indiana, and she has a friend in ten-year-old Marcy Frazier, a Cystic Fibrosis poster representative.

"Cheryl is like a big sister," Marcy said proudly. "And, every time I come here, I really feel like I'm entering the land of Oz."

Like Cheryl, Marcy also sees something beyond the entertainment. In *The Wizard of Oz* there is an enduring message. "Like, if you think you really don't care for yourself, you do have some special qualities. Everybody does," said Marcy.

"If happy little bluebirds fly. . . ."

The Wizard of Oz was released in 1939. In the half century since, it has been watched by legions of young and old alike. And, this delightful movie has given us all something we need—inspiration and courage.

"Why? Oh why can't I?"

 **RAY'S UPDATE: Cheryl is the creator of a nationally marketed children's fitness program, *Adventures in Oz with Cheryl*. Marcy is now married with a little girl of her own.**

Christmas Sharing

Birdie Whiteside   December 1989

One by one, little packets of candy are wrapped and put into a basket. One by one, the baskets are filled and a red bow is fastened to one side. The busy hands never stop. This is the stuff Christmas is made of. Not the confection. That's just a small part of it. It's these people who give their time to deliver Christmas, a dozen of them or so, seated at long tables in the conference center at Mount Zion Baptist Church in Indianapolis. And it's this woman. "Hello girls. How are you feeling this morning?" asks Birdie Whiteside, who started all this thirty-six years ago. On her own she made ten or fifteen of these little packages and took them to shut-ins.

Nowadays, the money for the gifts and wrappings is donated, and Birdie has about a hundred volunteers who visit seventy-nine nursing homes, an assortment of penal institutions, hospitals, and any number of people who are old, sick, or just lonely at Christmas.

So, why does she continue doing what she has done year after year, every

Christmas since 1953?

"Well, there's a joy in it," says Birdie. "There's a joy that you cannot explain. Because, when I go in to see the people they give me something as much as I give them. They give me a smile. That's very important and when I get through doing this I've had my Christmas."

At seventy-nine years old, Birdie moves slower than she used to. Wearing a light blue cloth coat and slippers that softly scuff the ground, she takes her gifts across the parking lot to a nearby nursing home. Birdie says she will do this as long as she has a gift to give.

The plain water pipe handrail helps as she labors on the steps, and then she is in the main room surrounded by residents, their own Christmas memories rekindled by Birdie's version of "Silent Night."

"Sleep in heavenly peace," to which she adds her own smile.

"All they need to know is somebody cares," Birdie tells me. "Somebody came to see them and somebody speaks a word of care to them. It doesn't take anything. Don't take much but a little time."

Birdie Whiteside gave a little more time today and in so doing gave something of herself, the warmest gift of all.

Birdie waved good-bye and called out, "Have a merry, merry Christmas."

Someone asked, "Birdie? Will you be back?"

"Yes, I will. I'll be back sometime," she said.

Owen Hansen

The first "Hans Glances" appeared in the *Lebanon Reporter* back in April 1959. Owen Hansen has written his way into a fifth decade now, taking potshots at the powerful and lending support to those who need it.

"I think every small town ought to have a curmudgeon type person like me to keep people honest," says Owen. "And, also, there's things that aren't hard news that people will call me about and I've never once awakened in the morning and felt like it was going to be a job to go to. It was always a pleasure to come here."

Over the years Owen has provided local angles to such stories as the John F. Kennedy assassination and even went to Vietnam in 1968 where he took a snapshot of some war-weary children. To this day he wonders what happened to them.

His ideas come from telephone tips, cards and letters, and networking with other writers.

Today, the shuttle launch was the major national story, but Owen's column will reflect some other items. Currently, he has been sniping at the Boone

County Commissioners whom he calls Larry, Curley, and Moe. But, he has been at odds with the commissioners before.

"In 1973 I got in a hassle with the commissioners and one of the guys said 'Well, hell, why don't you run if you know it all.' So, I ran and damn if I didn't win and get elected," says Owen. "I served one term and then I got out because of illness. The voters were sick of me. Ha, ha, ha."

Owen has a typewriter handy and, in fact, prefers the old clackity-clack days. But, he now uses a computer to fire away at the mighty with one notable exception.

"It's never been written," he says with some hesitation. "But we have one sacrosanct area here and that's Dan Quayle. His family owns our paper. But, never, ever has anybody told me what I can or can't write and that means a lot too, you know."

"But, do you ever beat up on him in your column?"

"No. I don't. I didn't come in on the turnip truck yesterday. Ha, ha, ha, ha."

"Hans Glances," as humorous as Owen is in person, appears three times a week, and he says if there's one thing that keeps it going it is that he is always honest. Although he admits, and we'll say it here publicly, he cheats at golf.

 **RAY'S UPDATE: Owen retired in 1995. For the past eight years, he has worked for the Boone County Sheriff's Department as a process server.**

Saint Patrick's Day Fire

March 1990

Fighting fires is one of the most dangerous jobs there is. Today, though, it is a lot safer than it used to be because of the extensive training firefighters undergo.

By the time a fire department recruit completes a sixteen-week course, he or she is schooled in strategy, hydraulics, hazardous materials, and emergency medical treatment.

But a century ago there was no training at all. A new fireman learned as he went along and fought fires on equipment that, while primitive by today's standards, was considered state of the art then.

It was about three o'clock in the afternoon on Saint Patrick's Day, March 17, 1890, when a fire broke out at the Bowen-Merrill Bookstore at 18 West Washington Street in Indianapolis.

The alarm was sounded and men rushed from their jobs to battle the flames. They were volunteers—office workers, a bank clerk, an attorney, a blacksmith. Others rushed into the street to see it all, called from their daily routine by an emergency.

Before long the blaze had escalated to a general alarm fire, bringing about sixty men with twenty horse-drawn wagons, including a couple of steam pumpers. Others were called to the street by the clamor, the sound of horses' hooves, bells clanging, whistles blowing, and men shouting.

Thousands of gallons of water were put on the four-story building, and soon the firefighters got the best of the fire. Or, so they thought. It re-ignited around five o'clock.

As Indianapolis Fire Department historian Captain Greg Roembke tells the story, the firefighters again doused the building with water. "And with that being a publishing company and all the paper goods and everything that was soaking up the water and the weight it created, at about 5:30 the whole thing just collapsed," says Roembke.

Twelve firemen were killed instantly when the floors pancaked one atop the other, and a thirteenth man died a couple of weeks later. The disaster meant that 20 percent of the men on the 1890 Indianapolis Fire Department had died.

Condolences poured in from around the nation, along with donations amounting to $52,000. Some of the money was used for burial expenses or medical bills for the injured. The rest of it was used to establish trust funds for the widows and children left in mourning. That trust fund was the beginning of the Indianapolis Fire Department pension system.

Today [1990], there is no monument to those who lost their lives in the worst tragedy in the history of the Indianapolis Fire Department. There is only a list of names on a plaque in the rotunda of the Indiana Statehouse and a similar marker at the site of the fire.

Of the men, we know little. There are apparently no living relatives here in Indiana of those who lost their lives. All we know is that they died in the line of duty on Saint Patrick's Day in 1890.

 **RAY'S UPDATE: In 1873 Daniel Glazier became the Indianapolis Fire Department's first fatality. His son, Ulysses Glazier, was one of those killed seventeen years later in the Saint Patrick's Day fire.**

Ryan White

April 9, 1990

At a time when any youngster would look ahead with anticipation, Ryan White was given a terrible burden.

He was only thirteen when he was told he would die of an incurable disease: Acquired Immune Deficiency Syndrome (AIDS).

It would have been extraordinarily difficult for anyone, but Ryan grew to maturity beyond his years and showed how remarkable a young man he was.

AIDS is an illness that takes away the body's ability to fight infection, but Ryan began a battle that would earn our respect, our admiration, and in the end our love.

Although he knew he would eventually lose his own fight to live, he confronted ignorance and fear and he won.

He became a teacher whose lessons were given in different forums: classrooms, when invited in; seminars, when asked to speak; and at news conferences and uncounted interviews. There was even a television movie based on his experiences.

With a limit set on his own life, he fought for the lives of others by becoming an international spokesman for AIDS research.

He walked with the stars. He was a statesman, a teenager who met with presidents. All of that in only five years.

It would be safe to say that everyone was touched by the news on Sunday that Ryan was gone, and there were countless tears, many shed in private places.

Ryan White came into all of our lives as a young man, barely a teenager, but he left a hero.

 **RAY'S UPDATE: This was our "Indiana's Own" on WISH-TV the day after Ryan passed away of AIDS on April 8, 1990. He was eighteen.**

Sammy Lee Davis

April 1990

The Congressional Medal of Honor is the highest military decoration the nation can bestow. It was presented for "conspicuous gallantry" to Sammy Lee Davis in 1969 by President Lyndon Johnson at a White House ceremony. A photograph of the event will be displayed at the Mooresville Public Library along with a bronze bust of Sammy by Chicago artist Robert Buono when the needed funds are raised.

David Blunk of the Mooresville Veterans of Foreign Wars Post 1111 is chairman of the committee to honor Sammy, and he explains that all of this is because of what happened on the night of November 18, 1967.

"It was in what they call the Plain of Reeds in the Mekong Delta near Cai Lay, Vietnam, which was about thirty miles west of Saigon," says Blunk.

Under enemy fire, Sammy suffered multiple wounds and broken vertebrae in his back. In spite of his injuries, he crossed the river under fire, picked up three wounded comrades, and, with one over his shoulders and one under each arm, he made his way back.

One of those he rescued was Jim Deister from Salina, Kansas. "Actually, I was an unwilling participant in all this," says Deister. "I just laid there. I had been shot in the head and chest and had multiple wounds and all that I knew about the battle for many years was that I had been across the river and that I had survived—somehow."

For twenty years Deister wondered who had saved his life and then, in 1988, he was reading a book about Medal of Honor recipients and came across a story about Sammy Lee Davis and an incident on the Plain of Reeds.

"It got more interesting when Sammy saw a black man across the river yelling for help and he came across the river and he found three of us," Deister notes. "The story mentioned that one was shot in the head. Right away my heart jumped. I said, 'Do you suppose this could be?'"

It was. The man who had saved his life was Sammy Lee Davis.

"I think about Sammy every day," says Deister, "and I think about the sacrifices that he made on my behalf."

Sammy Lee Davis left for Vietnam not long after he graduated from Mooresville High School. And today he returned. He had no idea that he would be honored in a special convocation. The school gymnasium was filled to capacity. Sammy remarked that it was an honor to have served his country, and the following day he served as grand marshal of the Mooresville Loyalty Day Parade.

George Mikelsons

May 1990

George Mikelsons has wanted to fly ever since he was a boy. It was his passion, to soar above it all. Now he does.

Piloting his private helicopter to his office, George looks down at the Indianapolis International Airport and the headquarters of the largest airline of its kind catering primarily to vacation travel and military charters. The airline is American Trans Air.

George buys jetliners like the Boeing 757 at a price of about $60 million apiece. It is the newest addition to a growing fleet of planes that includes twenty-two jet aircraft that today crisscross the oceans of the world.

In seventeen years he has guided a company to annual revenues of about $350 million. It is the story of a self-made man who was born in Latvia and displaced by World War II.

"During World War II," George recalls, "I became totally enamored by aviation. I was on the ground and watching the bombers and fighters doing their thing above Germany and I thought, 'My God, how much better to be up there than down here.'"

After the war George wound up in Australia, where he remained for eleven years.

He came to Indianapolis in 1960 and within a year he had his commercial pilot's license. In 1965 he signed on as pilot with a local travel club, Voyager 1000. Eight years later he decided to strike out on his own. "In 1973 I started with one airplane," George remembers. "It was a rusty old Boeing 720, which is the predecessor to the 707 airplane."

And so, American Trans Air was born.

In those early days, with a staff of only sixteen people, everyone did everything—from painting the plane to promoting flights, flying passengers to the islands and back, and doing it again for seven days a week.

The intimacy of a small staff is something George misses. He knew everyone's name. Today, it's just too big. ATA has a payroll of more than two thousand people, ranging from maintenance and aircraft crew to administrative staff and world radar tracking of the company's planes.

For all the growth, George says he never had a business plan and still doesn't to this day. "We made the decision just for the next year and the next year one brick upon the other until it got to this size but it's not by planning," he says. "It's not by design."

To George Mikelsons, flying was only something he dreamed of as a child. What he sees now has far exceeded that dream.

"Certainly. Beyond my wildest expectations," he says. "I never had any vision of grandeur for myself personally or the airline so I'm extremely happy and grateful for the accomplishments of the airline and I never expected to get to this point."

 RAY'S UPDATE: Semi-retired for a time, George returned to ATA in August 2002 to help his airline out of its financial struggle following the September 11, 2001, terrorist attacks on America. Today he serves as chairman and chief executive officer of the nation's tenth largest passenger carrier (based on revenue passenger miles).

American Cabaret Theatre

Claude McNeal   June 1990

For the past two years work has moved along quietly on the restoration of a grand old hall at the Athenaeum Turners, which dates to Indianapolis in the late 1890s. It's a so-called sympathetic renovation of the ballroom. It won't be exactly as it was, but it will have the same nineteenth-century ambiance.

The man with the vision is Claude McNeal, artistic director of the American Cabaret Theatre. "When I walked into this space, although it was run-down, it just hit me," says Claude. "It's the perfect space for what we do I've ever seen anywhere in the world."

In the past seventeen years, Claude has produced more than twenty original works that have been performed from New York to London, from New Haven, Connecticut, to French Lick, Indiana, and Indianapolis.

The process of restoring this hall has itself been a major production involving more than two hundred thousand dollars in grants from the Lilly Endowment, the Lilly Foundation, the Clowes Fund, and the Indianapolis Foundation. Union labor has been donated, and there has been major corporate support. Claude adds, "We have twenty-seven companies and organizations that have put in—we haven't added up the hours. Just tons of hours."

This historic hall is the perfect setting for the Cabaret—an intimate theatre atmosphere in which to make political and social statements as entertainment.

"It's going to be a dazzling theatre," Claude predicts. "I've done theatres in the major cities of the world and this is going to be as good as any."

There is usually a small army of workers here in the hall: carpenters, plasterers, electricians. Today there is only one, but timing is everything in theatre and this project is on time.

 RAY'S UPDATE: The American Cabaret Theatre, which celebrated its thirteenth season at the Athenaeum in 2003, is still going strong with its mainstage performances and educational programs. Claude's original cabaret shows have also been seen in Florida, Montana, Washington, Missouri, and Canada.

Wedding

Bill and Gladys   September 1990

They got settled in their chairs, talking softly, expectantly. The time had come. The organist began "The Wedding March."

And here comes Gladys Cameron. She is seventy-nine, and today she's getting married to her boyfriend Bill Rader. He's eighty-five.

The Reverend Joseph Wilkins begins, "Dearly beloved, we are gathered here today. . . ."

Among those who gathered today were other residents and staff at the Marion County Health Care Center in Indianapolis, about fifty witnesses in all.

Reverend Wilkins: "Please repeat after me. I, William Rader."

"I, William Rader," he repeats, as Gladys looks over and smiles.

Bill was a maintenance man here when he met Gladys back in 1941. They've been dating ever since.

As Gladys repeats, "to be my wedded husband," Bill smiles back.

Bill and Gladys decided fifty years of going steady was enough and now they will be married, each for the first time. Bill, smartly dressed in his dark suit and tie, Gladys, in white and pink with a blue bouquet.

Reverend Wilkins: "'Til death do us part."

Gladys: "'Til death do me part."

"What God has joined together let no one put asunder. Give her a kiss, Bill."

He did, and Gladys leaned her head on his shoulder and wept. We all did.

And, so, a man and woman who have seen more of this world than most have decided to spend the rest of their time together.

This is a day to remember. Tuesday, September 18, 1990, when Gladys and Bill became Mr. and Mrs. Rader in a love story the likes of which you'll never see again.

Tanks a Lot

Fred Ropkey   October 1990

Let's take a tour of Fred Ropkey's place. Greeting you in the front yard is a twenty-ton tank gun turret. Look beyond and you'll see an A-4 Skyhawk jet fighter, a T-33 jet trainer, a telescoping radar tower, a portable military control tower, and a Regulus rocket. In the pond behind his house there's an Apollo space capsule. Then there are the tanks—more than fifty of them. In addition, there are dozens of other vehicles, from vintage military motorcycles to jeeps and trucks and armor, and more jeeps, more tanks and motorcycles and tanks, and they all belong to Fred.

In classic understatement, Fred chuckles, "Essentially, my hobby is something that has really got completely out of control."

Fred Ropkey's hobby has evolved into the Indiana Museum of Military History, a superb collection of military weapons both domestic and foreign. Standing alongside a Soviet-built armored car captured during the 1967 Arab-Israeli war, museum curator Fred Warvel explains that it takes a full-time staff of six people to restore and preserve this history.

"In a hundred years from now, two hundred years from now, they'll be antiques and the world war will be to people then what the Civil War or the Revolutionary War is to us these days," says Warvel.

The cost of all this is enormous. For example, Fred has a World War II M-10 tank that wound up in the Middle East, where it was recently found by Fred, himself a former Korean War tank commander.

"The cost to ship that back and ship it from the Port of Haifa and to purchase the basic machine was forty-five thousand dollars," Fred explains. "We've been rebuilding that vehicle for over two years."

When finished, the M-10 may be worth two hundred thousand dollars and it will run like new, although as with all of the pieces in the collection the firing mechanisms have been disabled.

You may have seen some of Fred's collection in the movie, *Tank*, starring James Garner, or in *The Blues Brothers* film and assorted commercials.

But the purpose of the museum, Fred points out, is to preserve history—to save some of the military equipment men used in battle to preserve our freedom.

 **RAY'S UPDATE: Fred remains hard at work restoring military vehicles. His current project involved returning to operational condition a U.S. Navy River Patrol Boat from the Vietnam War.**

Brooklyn Dodger

Carl Erskine   April 1991

The Brooklyn Dodgers may have been the most colorful team in baseball. They certainly caught your eye. The organization led the drive for integration in big-league baseball by fielding a young black man named Jackie Robinson. And although they had failed to win a World Series in seventy-five years, they remained the beloved "bums" to their fans.

One person who was there, in the middle of it all, was "Indiana's Own" Carl Erskine.

Carl is an executive with Star Financial Bank in his hometown of Anderson. He knew nothing about banking in 1964, he says, but he knew lots of people who knew him. They remembered his time in the big leagues, as he does. He loves to reminisce. "I can recall that for two or three years after I got out of baseball," says Carl, "I'd catch myself all day long looking at my watch and saying, 'Well, let's see the guys are in spring training. Right now it's eleven fifteen. Pitchers will be going over to the string area.'"

Carl was barely out of high school when he was scouted by the Dodgers, signed a contract with the team, was sent to Fort Worth, and then to Brooklyn and Ebbetts Field. "I heard somebody in line, waiting for tickets as I walked through the rotunda trying to find the clubhouse," Carl recalls. "He said, 'Hey, dah goes da kid from Foyt Woyt.' That was my first exposure to Brooklyn and the first time I heard my name pronounced Cahl Oyskin, which they shortened to Oysk."

Oysk played for ten seasons in Brooklyn and when the jet plane made it possible to play on both coasts, the Dodgers abandoned Brooklyn for Los Angeles. Ebbetts Field was torn down.

Before he left, however, Carl and teammates Robinson, Duke Snyder, Gil Hodges, Pee Wee Reese, Roy Campanella, and all the rest gave Brooklyn its first and only World Series Championship.

"To win it in '55 was, you know, darn near a spiritual experience," says Carl. "I mean it was beyond exhilaration. When the last out, Reese to Hodges, was registered and we were national champions, we went in the clubhouse and, as I recall, it was rather quiet. These seasoned veteran players went in there, not throwing their gloves in the air and their hats, but, I think they were kind of in a prayerful attitude. How thankful we are to claim this crown, finally."

Outside on the streets a grateful fan echoed the thoughts in every neighborhood in Brooklyn: "I'm thrilled the Dodjas finally won. Three cheas for the Dodjas."

After his baseball career ended, Carl, at the age of thirty-two, enrolled in college as a freshman. He coached baseball at Anderson College and, with his wife Betty, taught his oldest son Jimmy to live with Down's syndrome. But, most will remember the man from Anderson who went to Brooklyn as a twenty-game winner in 1953, pitched a World Series no hitter that same year, and in one game struck out fourteen New York Yankees. To the fans of a team that was, Carl Erskine will always be number 17. And, he will always be Oysk.

RAY'S UPDATE: Retired as president of Star Financial Bank, Carl still serves on the bank's board. He remains active with Special Olympics and other community projects. Carl recently sold the family farm in Anderson to make way for a new school that will be named Erskine Elementary.

The Dollhouse

Vivian Allison   July 1991

Vivian Allison's dollhouse never looked so nice. There's some new furniture now, and the house itself has been painstakingly restored.

Although it has been vandalized numerous times, Vivian's dollhouse has survived on the same spot in the Connersville Cemetery since 1899.

Darrell Maines is one of those who has cared enough to come out and periodically repair the house. "There's not a lot of history that we know," says Maines. "What we understand is that the little girl wanted a dollhouse, and as the father was constructing it, she got sick and passed away. So, the father decided to complete the dollhouse and use it as a grave marker."

Most headstones and monuments mark a death and stand gray and cold, even in the sunshine. But one colorful fantasy, a dollhouse, tells us of a life, of Vivian Allison, age five.

Joyce Baker is another person who keeps the dollhouse as Vivian would have liked it. "I've always wondered if she was a . . . blue-eyed, blond-haired little girl, or a brown-eyed, brown-haired little girl," says Baker. "How big she was, you know, what things in life she would have liked?"

Vivian, who never saw her dollhouse, would certainly have enjoyed it. That's what the small group of about twenty townspeople thought, too. That's why they have put it back the way it was.

The house has curtain-lined windows on all four sides. Inside you'll see a small, four-poster bed, a table with a tiny mirror, a few pictures on the wall, a wagon, and a doll—all the things a little girl would need to play house.

Louis Brochman peeked inside with me and marveled, "This was all hand carved. The posts were turned, hand turned, every one, and they had to spend quite some time to do this, and it must have been a real love for their daughter to accomplish this."

No one knows how many times Horace and Carrie Allison came to visit this place before they came to rest forever beside their daughter, just one of the hundreds who lie here now, remembered by no one and drawing only the curious.

RAY'S UPDATE: Vivian apparently died of something easily treated today, appendicitis. The Allison family of Connersville, like most, came and went and were soon forgotten. The last I heard a distant relative of Allison, the only one left, lived in Florida. In an interview years ago, she said the family always talked about the little girl and her dollhouse. You can see Vivian's dollhouse at the cemetery on State Road 9 near Tenth Street in Connersville.

The Stickman

Nixon S. Elliott   August 1991

There are thousands of people at the Indiana State Fair every day. But I'd like you to meet just one. His name is Nick.

"You got Polish and Eye Talian sausages," he cries out, his shouted message tempting the noisy crowds. "It's dinner time, come on. They're so good, so big. Just look how big they are."

Nixon S. Elliott. Eighty years old. He's been around fairs in Ohio, Michigan, and Indiana since he was three.

Fair workers such as Nick are called troopers, and they have a language all their own. Concessions are called joints, people who duke the customers or bring them in are called stickmen. The stickman at this food joint tells everybody within earshot about the whole meal in a biscuit.

"Whole meal in a biscuit here," Nick intones. "Whole meal in a biscuit."

Oh, if you could hear his sausage serenade. His barker's cadence would bring you right in.

"Get your Polish and Italian sausages. They're so good you'll like 'em all right. So good you'll like 'em all right," Nick calls.

Nick has sung the praises of the food joints longer than he can remember. It all started back when drinks were kept cool in iceboxes and kerosene lanterns offered flickering light brightened by shiny reflectors.

His father was a trooper, too, and Nick went with him to work. When he got tired, he fell asleep under the counter behind the apron. Fast asleep to the sound of music from the midway and the persistent calls of the stickmen.

An old man now, Nick can still sing his bedtime lullaby: "Fried onions, peppers, spices. Whole meal in a biscuit."

Nick works sometimes fourteen or sixteen hours a day. He cleans and polishes, and he is an employer's dream come true.

Ronnie Smith, who owns the sausage joint, says, "He motivates the others, because he outworks them all. The young ones, middle aged, and the old ones. He outworks them all."

Across the walkway is Art Carrol, the Elephant Ear man. "I'm not a young man," Carrol says. "I'm sixty-two years old Ray, but I think about him whenever I get up in the morning, and when I'm tired I think, 'Boy, ole Nick, he's going, why can't you Art?' Ha, ha, ha."

So how does Nick do it? "When I get up of a morning, I drink a glass of warm water and a cup of coffee for each leg. Get up, ready to go," he says.

"There ain't a stiff bone in my body but one. No arthritis. No rheumatism."

Nick was quite the dashing fellow back in 1930. Some things change in sixty years and some don't. Nick is still at the fair, still a stickman and still duking the customers.

"Well, come in if you're hungry," Nick calls out to fairgoers. "I got your dinner all ready. Hey, look how big they are."

 **RAY'S UPDATE: At last word Nick was still bringing them in at the age of ninety-two.**

Sharecropper's Daughter

Jennie Whittaker   September 1991

It's said to be the largest log structure in the State of Tennessee. It's called Wynnewood. Built in the early 1800s near Nashville, it was a stagecoach stop, a resort, and hotel. It was where Jennie Whittaker of Indianapolis grew up.

"I was with my mother as a little girl, two or three years old, because she worked there, see?" she remembers.

Jennie was the youngest of eleven children. Her grandparents and great-grandparents were slaves. Her mother died when she was five. Her father worked as a sharecropper, and Jennie has taken those memories of her childhood and put them into a song.

"It's about the beginning of my life," she says. "I was born a sharecropper's daughter in the foothills of old Tennessee."

The lyrics of her song continue: "And, my playground was in the backyard of the rich man, but I was just as happy as I could be. My mother, she worked for a living. . . ."

Jennie sang her song this summer during the Wynnewood Festival, and she told me people came from all over Tennessee. To sing her song at the festival was "exciting," she says. "It was so exciting, and everybody seemed to enjoy it so."

Jennie went to work at Wynnewood when she was nine doing what her mother, grandmother, and great-grandmother had done: she swept the floors, cleaned the rooms, made the meals, and washed the dishes, making at the most two dollars a week. She left for Indianapolis when she was eighteen.

Wynnewood has a rich history, whose guests included Andrew Jackson and Sam Houston. Wynnewood's history also includes an eighty-year-old Indianapolis woman—Jennie Whittaker, the sharecropper's daughter.

"Yes," she sings, "my playground was in the backyard of the rich man, but I was just as happy as I could be."

Lloyd and Floyd Newkirk

January 1992

"We walk alike. Talk alike."

An eighth-grade English class in New Castle is learning how commercials are made. The students are learning how from two of television's newest stars, Lloyd and Floyd.

Lloyd: "We walk alike."

Floyd: "Talk alike."

Lloyd: "Even eat the same kind of chips."

Lloyd and Floyd Newkirk are Indiana born and raised, and they're just back from filming a corn-chip commercial in California.

Lloyd: "Just relax."

Floyd: "Now, here's what they tell you out in Hollywood, 'Relax. We're here to have fun.'"

And that's exactly what the producer who hired them wanted, identical twins, sixty-five or older, who are still kids and have fun.

Lloyd and Floyd had to try on forty-seven different outfits before a wardrobe was selected. As a memento, they were given a copy of the original script.

After their schoolroom visit, I got to know them a little better.

Lloyd: "Being twins is a kick."

Floyd: "We've been tricking people for years."

They tricked their teachers in school by switching seats and even switched dates once while out with identical twin girls.

Floyd: "We decided that we'd switch on them while we were out, and they decided that they'd switch on us and the way it happened is they happened to switch at the same time we switched on them, so we were still with the same one."

Ray: "Did anybody know?"

Floyd: "Nobody knew 'til the next day."

Nobody will believe this coincidence, but after the school visit we went to a nearby diner and a set of identical twins, Mary and Martha, sat down at another table.

"I guess there's twins everywhere," Floyd quips.

Maybe, but there is only one Lloyd and Floyd. Or is it two?

The Newkirk brothers were the only twins in a family of sixteen children. They've both been married for fifty years, and both were born seventy years ago on Saint Valentine's Day.

Floyd lives in Carmel now, and Lloyd lives in Lebanon. Or, is it the other way around? Anyway, that's the kind of thing you find yourself muttering after you spend some time with Lloyd and Floyd, two of "Indiana's Own."

 RAY'S UPDATE: Now eighty-one years old, the twins are the oldest such pair as part of an Indiana University study of twins. Lloyd stays busy golfing and has written a book about his life, while Floyd drives for Lebanon's senior services department and repairs and paints houses.

Jim Davis

Who would have thought that a lazy, cynical, mischievous fat cat would capture so many smiles?

Who would have thought? Certainly not Jim Davis. "Yes," he says, "I'm surprised by the growth. I had no idea. I had hoped to be able to increase the syndication and someday have a book and maybe someday down the road, about now, have a TV show or a doll or something."

A television show? Jim has won four Emmys, and *Garfield and Friends* is just entering a sixth season on Saturday mornings. A doll or something? How about more than four thousand dolls or something?

On every possible object on which Garfield might appear, there he is, including three dozen books. All of this because of one cat.

"Garfield's first appearance in the newspaper was June 19, 1978, in forty-one newspapers," Jim says. "We're in over twenty-three hundred now worldwide, so he's enjoying quite a bit of growth."

In the beginning, he continues, "Garfield was almost somber. But, he changed over the years. Today, Garfield's eyes are bigger, his ears smaller, his mouth wider, and his legs longer."

Garfield's home is Paws, Inc., just outside of Muncie. There are forty employees working to create and market various products. There are also several cartoonists who prepare Jim's sketches for the printer.

Sitting at a five-foot easel with sketch pad, Jim tells us how he works: "The most important thing I do is the comic strip. So, I still do the comic strip. I do all the writing. The humor has to emanate from the comic strip. That feeds the rest of the program. So, I stay close to the things where I feel I'm of some worth. Ha, ha, ha, ha."

There are a couple of main reasons for Garfield's success. He has universal appeal—everyone everywhere can identify. The other is the fellow in Middle America who knows, Jim Davis, the guy with the sketch pad and the gags.

When he was a boy on his Indiana farm, Jim loved to draw. His family had about two dozen cats, and so he drew cats. Today, one of those cats is an international celebrity, but Garfield doesn't know he's so famous. "It's better that way," says Jim.

RAY'S UPDATE: America's favorite lasagna-loving feline celebrated his twenty-fifth anniversary on June 19, 2003. Today the *Garfield* comic strip is the most widely syndicated in the world, appearing in 2,750 newspapers with an estimated daily readership of 263 million. The first-ever Garfield movie is in development with 20th Century Fox with an expected release near Christmas 2003.

National Hot Rod Association Champ

Bob Glidden   September 1992

One of the greatest pro stock racing teams in the world is a family affair. It began twenty-seven years ago when Bob Glidden met Etta while cruising in his Ford hot rod on the west side of Indianapolis.

As Bob recalled, "Etta and I raced on local race-tracks on weekends just to have fun, and the more we did it the more we enjoyed it. And then the five-dollar trophies turned into small purses and the small purses turned into bigger purses."

They never suspected that those weekend races would produce the great-est driver in the sport, the winner of ten world championships who can also point to an unequaled eighty career victories.

Bob would be the first to tell you he wouldn't be anywhere without his fans. The least he could do is sign an autograph. Well, he signs ninety thou-sand autographs a year. Wherever the Glidden team goes, fans line up to say hello and go away with a signed program or an autographed photo.

And now Bob and Etta's two sons are racing. Does she worry? "I never really gave it much thought until Bob had a wreck in 1986," she says. "And, it was a pretty severe wreck and now it always seems to be with me."

Bob and Etta's sons love the racing circuit too. Billy is up from Houston for the nationals, and Rusty is taking the Motorcraft backup car onto the track along with the Glidden name.

"Everything I do and everything I am I owe to my mom and dad," says Rusty.

"It's great, you know," says Bob. "I think it's so great to see our own kids out here participating."

Bob Glidden lives in the town where he grew up, Whiteland, Indiana. He says that when he was a boy, his family was too poor to pay attention, and he never forgets that even though he's spent much of his life in the fast lane.

"A lot of people when they make the big time so to speak, they forget where they come from. And, I think that's why we've got such a fan following," Bob observes. "I don't feel that I'm any different right now than I was twenty or twenty-five years ago. I might be a lot older and a lot tireder but that would be about it."

The Final Edition

Mel Hiller January 28, 1993

His fingers work the keyboard like the newspaper-man he has been for the past forty-five years. His name is Mel Hiller, and he sits before a relic of journalism, the Linotype, at one time the heartbeat of just about every newspaper in the world.

Long before entire pages could be set with copper plates, each story had to be literally pounded out in molten lead one letter at a time.

"They're really a workhorse," Mel says. "They have a lot of little parts. But, if you take care of them, they'll serve you well."

Modern papers use computers with keyboards that speak in clicks. Mel prefers the clanking and hissing of the Linotype with its assemblers and lead heated to 536 degrees Fahrenheit and the stories that come out ready for the press in full lines of type, hence the name.

Today, Mel is preparing the final edition of the *Jamestown Press*, the last issue for a weekly newspaper that first appeared in 1873.

Mel's father Harold was also a newspaperman who set his first type when he was only nine years old and ran the press for thirty-one years. Mel took over when he was twenty. Now, he's getting tired. "I've had one week's vacation in forty-five years so this will give me a little free time," says Mel.

Jamestown has a population of about nine hundred. For more than a century the people here got their news from the *Press*. So many stories, such as the time about forty years ago when a jewelry salesman was held up just outside of town and robbed of a quarter of a million dollars worth of gems. Mel remembers like it was yesterday: "That happened on a Thursday and we had already gone to press. But, we burned those papers of what we had run and got the story out."

On every Thursday there was news from the town board or the school board. Townsfolk got to read all about it.

One lady tells me, "Mr. Hiller always attended all of those meetings, and that's going to be a big loss so I don't know how we'll keep up with it."

Another reader remarks, "It's going to be really weird. First thing my daughter does is to run over to the post office and get the paper and read all the gossip."

The nineteenth-century printing press produces one page at a time. The ink rollers blacken the Linotype letters, pull back, a sheet of paper drops into place, and on it goes until it's all done, folded, and there are nine hundred copies of the *Press*, one for everybody in town. The school menus, who died, and who got born. Now it has come down to this, the final edition of a newspaper that has not missed an issue, not one, in one hundred twenty years.

 RAY'S UPDATE: After the *Jamestown Press* closed, the old printing press was sold to a collector. One of the Linotype machines and much of the archives from the *Press* are today preserved in a museum in the same building where the paper was printed.

Ralph Teeter

March 1993

Look around his basement shop and you can see more than the man who worked here for more than fifty years. His name was Ralph Teeter, and he was blind. An accident took his eyesight when he was five years old, and yet he went on to become an engineer and run a company, Perfect Circle, that still produces piston rings.

He rubbed elbows with automaker Henry Ford, presidential contender Wendell Willkie, and radio commentator Lowell Thomas.

Ralph may have been blind but he loved to tinker. He made a steam engine when he was only twelve years old, and much later he invented something that everyone will recognize. He called it a speedostat.

Today, of course, we call it cruise control, something many would find impossible to live without on a long highway trip. It was made by Ralph *because* he was blind. As his daughter, Marjorie Meyer, explains, "Of course he didn't drive a car, so he rode with other people who complained that they would drive faster than they intended."

Feeling the car's acceleration and deceleration, Ralph thought it would be more comfortable to ride along at a constant speed. He sold his speedostat to automobile companies, who changed the name to cruise control.

Ralph held patents on more than a dozen other inventions developed in his shop, including a motorized riding mower and the automatic gearshift.

Although Ralph could feel the fine woodwork in his home he would never know the beauty of the stained glass windows. But no matter. It was his blindness that allowed him to see things others missed.

 **RAY'S UPDATE: Ralph was born in Hagerstown, Indiana, in 1890. He died in 1982.**

Baby Deer

July 30, 1993

"Here baby. Here baby."

You'll find Betty Mullis behind her country house calling Baby three times a day. She whistles again and repeats, "Here baby. Here baby."

It's thought that Baby was maybe a twin, the runt abandoned for some reason by her mother, and so the Mullis family took her in.

"It's kind of a two-man thing to feed her because she gets so excited about getting a ninny [bottle] that she'll just knock you down to get it," says Betty. "Oh boy. Here we go."

For the past three months Baby has been coming around for her bottle—four bottles at a time actually—that contains a mixture of condensed milk and water.

"We used to have to warm the milk, I used to warm it in the microwave, but she takes it cold now," says Betty.

As long as Baby hangs around she'll have a place to visit and play, and as far as the State of Indiana is concerned, it's OK so long as there's no fence.

Marlin Dodge, an Indiana conservation officer, makes it official: "In this case here, you can see the animal's not confined. You know, she's free to come in and out of the yard as she wants. So there's no violation ever occurring at this point."

At first Baby was invited inside with the family but the past few weeks she's been spending more and more time in the nearby woods.

"When I got her," says Betty, "she was a lot littler. She was so little. We figured she weighed about five pounds."

We watched in the warm afternoon sun as Baby played around with the Mullis children, age four and seven. She darted one way, then the next, and jumped and ran to the woods and sprinted back to the appreciative sound of giggles and laughter.

Baby is getting bigger by the day and she's been coming by a little less frequently. One of these days when something tells her it's time, Baby will go into the woods to stay. For a southern Indiana family and its guest, however, this has been a season to remember.

 **RAY'S UPDATE: The baby deer who visited is long gone, but Betty and her family continue to feed and care for the wildlife who often visit their home.**

Telephone Voice

Ann Craig   September 1993

Picking up the phone and dialing a number is so commonplace we scarcely give it another thought. In fact, that's how dialing mistakes are made and therein lies another story.

How often have you heard this? "We're sorry, it's not necessary to dial a 'one' or 'zero' and the area code when dialing this number. Please hang up and try again."

So, who belongs to that voice that so irritatingly tells you that you've done something wrong? Not some witchlike character with a rasping voice but someone quite the opposite. The person behind the message that always sounded so horrible until now is Ann Craig. Not only heard by telephone users but by thousands of listeners to Indianapolis radio station WENS. In the past five years she has recorded hundreds of messages for the telephone company, and on occasion she has wound up talking with herself.

"One time I called up the phone company with a question about my own phone bill and I got me telling me to hold and I'd be answered in the order in which I had been received, and I thought, 'This is really odd,'" says Ann.

"To reach customer assistance, please. . ."

So, the next time you dial incorrectly, this is the lady who owns the voice who apologizes for your mistake.

"We're sorry, you must first dial a 'one' or a 'zero.'. . ."

 **RAY'S UPDATE: Ann now co-hosts a morning show at WYJZ-FM Indianapolis and is partnered in a business with her husband.**

Mr. Cheap

Richard Stowe   August 1993

Richard Stowe has a yard sale every year. It's the mother of all yard sales. He had his first ten years ago and attracted so much attention he's had one every August since.

On his front lawn he has rows of tables set end to end, fifteen rows each about fifty feet long. Each covered with the items needed for a yard sale.

"Most everybody's happy," he explains while walking among the tables. "They bring the kids. Weekends we get fifteen hundred people out here. And, of course we show them where the soda is, the shade trees and the rest room. It's sort of like the country club of flea markets."

Richard, who calls himself Mr. Cheap, gets all this stuff by buying entire households following a divorce or death. He sells the larger items right away and saves the rest in his barn until August.

Buying and selling so many things, some valuables have slipped through his fingers, such as a wristwatch he sold to a guy a few years ago for a dollar that turned out to be worth five thousand.

He holds up a box for me to see. "You can find a phone answering machine complete for a dollar. You know? Complete from Radio Shack," he notes.

I wondered if a lot of people might look at this and ask, "Isn't this just so much junk?"

"One man's trash is another man's treasure," he tells me. "You can never say what's going to be junk. It's amazing. Everybody has a different definition."

Richard got into this business about twenty years ago. He wanted to work for himself. Every summer he sets up shop in his front yard and sells a year's worth of stuff at two dollars a paper-sack full.

"Now, here's a bag. Whose bag is this?" Richard asks. He holds it high over his head. "Look at this. An antique toaster, 1930s. Original antique toaster with the original plug. Yea."

The way Richard sees it, this is just an extension of a hobby he began when he was only nine years old. His boyhood hobby was collecting. "I collected rocks and coins," he says. "Yes, it makes life interesting."

Most every yard sale has as least a box or two of stuff. You know, an old, scratched forty-five rpm record, a bent screwdriver, one shoe, and a plastic knife. To some people, it's all in the hunt. To Mr. Cheap, it's a way of life.

 **RAY'S UPDATE: Mr. Cheap's yard sale continued until a few years ago when busy traffic on the road made parking dangerous. But, you'll still find him buying and selling at flea markets around central Indiana. You can't miss him.**

Wolf Park

Erich Klinghammer   August 1993

Spend a few hours with a wolf and the myths will vanish, as you'll discover on a visit to Wolf Park in Battle Ground, Indiana.

Dr. Erich Klinghammer founded the seventy-five acre park twenty years ago to study an animal once driven to near extinction in the lower forty-eight states. Even today, he acknowledges, there are some who believe that the wolf is a threat. "Much of the opposition comes from people who don't know much about the wolf," Erich explains. "You don't have to kill everything in sight. I mean, this is old nineteenth-century thinking that is outdated."

Erich's research focuses on the wolf-pack instinct and breeding, and his studies include the American bison and how they react in proximity to wolves.

There are seventeen buffalo in the park and about fifteen wolves, all of which have been raised in captivity. It costs about a hundred thousand dollars a year to operate Wolf Park. The money comes from grants and donations and through adoptions. Approximately two hundred fifty people from around the world have paid one hundred twenty-five dollars apiece to adopt a wolf. Each year some sixteen thousand people will come here to see the wolves and the man who studies them.

"What we like to do is, using the wolf as a magnet, to draw people in," says Erich. "We then talk about the role of the wolf in the ecosystem and say, 'Look, the wolf can live within its means in the wild. We as humans have to learn to live within our means on this planet.'"

If nothing else, the wolf is a survivor, having learned to get along in a hostile world. Today, there is perhaps no wild animal in North America with more friends than the wolf.

 **RAY'S UPDATE: Dr. Erich Klinghammer, Purdue University professor emeritus, served as a consultant on the program to reintroduce the timber wolf to Yellowstone National Park.**

Once a Globetrotter

Sonny Smith   September 1993

You never know who you'll run into at the supermarket. For example, I met Sonny Smith managing the meat counter at the Marsh store at Georgetown Road and Fifty-sixth Street in Indianapolis. At that time he had been in the food business for about thirty-six years.

But Sonny used to be in a different line of work. Once, he was a Harlem Globetrotter. He was recruited in 1948 by a Globetrotter scout, the legendary Jesse Owens. He tried out in Chicago and got the job.

Sonny was on the team from 1948 until 1957 and made good money in those years. About twelve hundred dollars a month, Sonny tells me, adding, "That was BIG money in those days."

Sonny also said life as a Globetrotter was far from glamorous. "Those days were tough, I tell you," he reminisces. "I'm glad that I went through those days. Truly. It was a great experience. But, there were many more experiences. A lot of times we had to ride at night, because there wasn't any place for us to sleep. We couldn't get a hotel room." Because they were black.

The Globetrotters used an instrumental recording of "Sweet Georgia Brown," by Brother Bones and The Shadows. Rhythm provided by clattering bones on the knee, the melody offered in a whistle. As the song played, the players bedazzled the crowd with their astounding ball handling and their humorous routines. Sonny was the guy who dribbled, while the other Globetrotters rested. He toured with Sammy Gee, Bob Hall, Carl Helums, and the incredible Goose Tatum. They played every year from November to April. In 1957 Sonny left the road for good and settled into another life.

Showtime ended many years ago, but sometimes, when it's quiet, Sonny Smith can still hear the music.

Amish Farm

The barn door opens with a clatter to let in the dawn. Several horses breathe heavily and shift their weight from side to side, knowing their day is about to begin. Munching on grain just put out, they offer no resistance to the leather harness. Within minutes a magnificent pair of Belgians is pulling a flatbed wagon through the early morning sunlight and out to the field.

This is how the day always begins on the Schmucker farm in northern Indiana's Allen County—with horses. The farm could not exist without them.

Martin Schmucker has lived here ever since his marriage to Amanda in 1959. In the years since, the couple has raised four sons, expanded the farm, and made its living from harvests and horse breeding (the Schmuckers own eighty Belgian horses).

Two hundred fifty acres are tilled with horsepower and fertilized with manure. One hundred twenty acres of the farm are devoted to vegetables, which are sold at the family's produce market. The market draws customers from Indiana, Ohio, Illinois, and Michigan.

The Schmuckers are descendants of French and Swiss settlers. German is the family language and the first language for children who attend school only through the eighth grade. The Amish are hard working, religious, and resourceful. They make their own clothing and most of their tools and equipment.

Martin is in his late fifties. He is stocky, his hands rough from hard work, his hair turning gray, his beard full and shaved across the top lip according to Amish tradition. A man grows a beard after he marries.

A large one-story building is set aside for drying and sorting the vegetables after they are harvested. We sat on a sorting table as Martin explained how his farm got started. "The ground or the property in this area is very, very expensive," he says. "So, back when we started, I was looking at something that I could make more dollars per acre, have less land, involve the whole family and that type of thing. We started out with a little card table in 1965."

As we talked the women in the family finished the laundry and prepared the noon meal. That done, I was given a privileged look inside an Amish home. Spartan by any standards, there are no adornments. There are no family photos on the wall, only quilted panels with the name of each family member. The Amish don't believe in likenesses. Also, there are no modern appliances. Heat is provided by wood or coal and illumination by gas lamps. The Amish say if you've never had electricity, you don't miss it. The simple surroundings match the family's simple lifestyle and friendly manner, which is almost disarming.

Different from most of us and yet, Amanda chuckles, "We're just people like you."

The Amish are like us in many ways except they have remained in a culture that is barely changed from the seventeenth century. We have seen them through our windshields in their traditional blue clothing and familiar hats. We look in admiration at their neatly kept farms and watch in childlike fascination at a buggy moving to the timeless cadence of hoofbeats.

The Schmuckers are but one of some fourteen hundred Amish families within a twenty-mile radius living a life of simplicity and grace along the back roads.

 **RAY'S UPDATE: The Schmucker Farm Market is located on Doty Road near the town of Milan Center in Allen County.**

Columbus Squires

Someone's final resting place in an old family plot can be forgotten in only a few generations, but a group of teenagers wants us to remember.

These are kids from the Greensburg area in Decatur County, and they have come together for a common purpose—to find old cemeteries and clean them.

We met at the end of a farm field. Just off the dirt road there is a small hill barely visible for the trees and brush. Youth counselor Jason Dwenger explains their mission: "There are 109 cemeteries in the county like this, little family plots, and it'll take a lot of time to get through all of them. We're hoping other groups will catch on to something like this. Right now, we've done four, but this summer is our first whole summer of doing this. We expect to get probably ten or twelve [done]."

They cut back the brush, chainsaw some small trees, and discover their first stone. One of the young people in the group leans down to read the faded inscription: "Edward J. Son of . . . somebody. Born July Third, 1845.

Age looks like two years. Yea, two years. Aawwwww."

Under the brush there are more weathered stones telling of people who came this way and left only their names for us to see. There's Sarah, the fifty-three-year-old wife of Thomas Fortune. She was born in 1798 and died in 1851.

As we gazed around at the newly cleared cemetery, Jason says, "I was thinking about it just a while ago, you know, we were cutting down with chain saws these little trees and stuff. When they cleared the land they cleared big trees and stumps and they had to do all that by hand and saws. It's unreal to think of the lifestyle that they've spent."

The half dozen kids here call themselves the Columbus Squires. They work a concession stand at the local Bingo game once a month to raise money for gasoline and chain-saw rental and, if they're lucky, they'll have enough money for the epoxy adhesive (a hundred dollars a gallon) needed to mend broken headstones.

"I'll tell you what," says Jason. "A lot of people think that our generation is a lot of vandals and we tear stuff up. I guess we're out to prove that wrong."

For a hundred years or so a man and woman and at least one child rested atop a small hill in the Indiana countryside, forgotten except for the weeds and wildflowers and the trees. Today, at last, somebody came by to pay respects.

 **RAY'S UPDATE: The young people of the Columbus Squires have since gone their own ways. But in their five years together they had cleaned up nearly thirty cemeteries**.

Tyree Coleman

March 1995

The local library has some competition these days in the form of a fifteen-year-old high school student. His name is Tyree Coleman, and he has done a remarkable thing. He has established his own lending library for kids in the neighborhood.

When he was six, Tyree led a demonstration of kids his age at the public apartments where he lived to demand a program that would offer them some activities.

"Now they have 'life planning' and 'youth councils' in every housing community and they say it's because of me and I'm happy about that," says Tyree.

Then, when he was twelve: "My mom had lost both her job and my father and so we had to move to a homeless shelter and while I was there, like the third day, I thought, 'Oh, this is pitiful. I'm not about to sit here and be bored again.'" So, he established a tutoring program with the support of the Mount Olive Crisis Care Center and tutored dozens of kids age four to ten.

Now he has a library at home, a brightly colored room filled with perhaps a thousand books and magazines.

"I have fiction, nonfiction. I have biographies, autobiographies," Tyree notes. "I have dictionaries. I have encyclopedias."

His accomplishments include a lending library, tutoring, and neighborhood programs for kids. And, he is all of fifteen years of age.

"I'm tired of seeing people out on the streets, 'cause I see it all the time," he says. "People who are drunks and drug addicts out on the streets and stuff and I see young people, even some of my ex-friends, strung out on drugs and I don't like to see people like that. So, if I can help somebody in any way, shape, or form I'm going to help them and hopefully they'll become better people."

 **RAY'S UPDATE: Tyree was an early winner of our We Value Youth Award, a Marsh-sponsored series that honored the accomplishments of young people for seven years running. In 2001 Tyree founded the not-for-profit Center for Hope, a shelter for homeless teens.**

Dewey's Dogs

March 1995

A couple of years ago Bill Dewey fell out of bed and was knocked unconscious. His two dogs lay with him on the floor, on either side, until he got up and called for help.

It was later, in the hospital, where Bill and I met. He started by telling me he was ninety-five. "Born in 1900," he said. Twelve years ago he lost his wife and now he's about to lose his dogs.

"And if I lay down to sleep, she'll lay on her back and the other one will lay on her side and we go to sleep," Bill said of his pets, Mary and Betty.

Bill has been hospitalized the past couple of weeks, and because he's unable to care for himself, he won't be going home.

"My sister, she's eighty-nine and she's got glaucoma in her eyes and wants me to come to Beech Grove in a nursing home and be with her. That's all we have left," Bill said. "And, she said we ought to be together just the few years we've got. So, that's where I'm going to go."

What will happen to his dogs? One of the Methodist Hospital nurses has offered to adopt Mary, and Betty will go to live with a friend of his family.

Before that happens though, Mary and Betty paid one last visit to their good friend. They jumped on Bill's lap and licked his face. He hugged them back. The time had come for Bill to say good-bye to the only really close friends he's had these past few years.

Captured in this moment are all the shared times, all the laughter, and the wagging tails for a tired old man and his dogs.

Owen County Artist

Ken Bucklew   July 1995

They say oil and water don't mix, but don't tell that to Ken Bucklew. Ken paints in oil, watercolors, and acrylics, and his work is outstanding.

His Owen County studio offers a wooded view. As he puts some final touches to a landscape he's working on, he tells me, "[I've] been influenced by the Hoosier Group of painters, T. C. Steele, J. Ottis Adams, and I forget the rest of their names, but this is kind of stylized after those early impressionistic paintings."

Like those artists who were here earlier, Ken prefers to capture nature. "It has a wilder look to it. Not everything is real close, accurate detail," he says. "You see here I'm not painting everything weed for weed, and flower for flower. You get the impression of it."

But impressionism is only one side of Ken's work. Look around his studio and you'll find maybe several different styles. His work appears on Christmas cards, Indiana game-bird stamps, the Indiana Department of Natural Resources calendar, and in homes across the land.

Ken is an obviously successful artist, and I was curious to learn where he studied. "I'm self taught," he says. "I studied commercial art and advertising at a vocational college down in Columbus back in the seventies and after that I worked for an ad agency for a few years. But for all of this, I'm totally self taught."

Although he specializes in nature, he doesn't call himself a wildlife artist or a landscape artist. He paints wildflowers, birds, beetles, landscapes, and, as he put it, "all kinds of critters."

In 1975 Ken was paralyzed from the neck down in a diving accident and had to learn how to walk and paint all over again. He has often wondered how different his life would be today if it had not been for his injury. "If I had never gotten hurt," he says, "I'd probably be doing something else right now for a living and just painting on the side as a hobby."

 **RAY'S UPDATE: Ken's studio is directly opposite the main entrance to McCormick Creek State Park in Owen County.**

Skydiver

Joe Weber   November 1995

Angel Falls lies in one of the most remote reaches of Venezuela. From a crest overlooking the falls, one can gaze out over a magnificent forest stretching to the horizon. There is a steady mist rising from the tumbling waters crashing on the rocks below.

Up to that crest stepped Joe Weber from Indianapolis. "I wanted to soak up the whole experience," he explains, his voice breathless as he relives the moment. "And, I had a camera on facing my feet and I hung my toes over the edge."

Joe is a skydiver about to do what few people have done before. He went to the edge and jumped. From three thousand feet, impact would be in twenty-one seconds. There is no time for a second parachute.

"There was about seven seconds before I had enough airspeed built up that I could fly away from the cliff. That's when everything really started to click in," says Joe. "The cliff started to move about one hundred twenty miles an hour about three feet behind me, and I was totally awestruck."

Subtle movements of his arms, hands, and legs allowed Joe to steer away from the cliff until fifteen seconds into his flight, when he deployed his chute at about seven hundred feet.

"It was absolutely spectacular," he says. "There is nothing in this world I could ever do to top this. I'll call it a vacation for me. I waited fifteen seconds before I deployed my chute, so I was really pushing it to try and get to the landing area. I came up only three feet short."

A former Special Forces paratrooper, Joe is now a skydiving instructor who has logged more than three hundred jumps this year alone, but nothing like this. "I had friends tell me this was just going to be another skydive because of the height," he says. "It's no skydive."

"So your dream has come true?" I ask.

"Yes it has. Absolutely."

"Now what?"

"Exactly. I think about that every day that I wake up."

While Venezuela may prohibit future jumps from Angel Falls there are other high places to tame, and more than likely Joe Weber will be there.

RAY'S UPDATE: Joe was a twenty-seven-year-old student at the Indiana University School of Dentistry at the time of his appearance on "Indiana's Own." Since our interview, he went into dental practice and continued his passion of jumping from fixed objects. One of his accomplishments was to jump from the world's tallest building in Kuala Lumpur in Malaysia to welcome the New Year in 2000.

Hiker

Jean Deeds May 1996

Been out for a walk lately? Bet it was nothing like the walk Jean Deeds took. Jean is among a select group of people who has hiked the Appalachian Trail from beginning to end.

Jean read about a woman who had done it and decided to do it for herself. She would have to hike 2,168 miles from Georgia to Maine, cross more than four hundred mountains, countless rivers and streams, and pass through fourteen states in all sorts of weather. She was forced to do it in two stages because within three hundred miles of the finish she fell between boulders, broke her leg, and had to return a year later to complete her journey.

Jean looked deep within to find a reason for such a monumental trek. "I think I wanted to get very far outside my comfort level and see what I was made of," she says. "And, I guess I needed something to shake up my life a little bit."

Restocking food along the way, she carried about sixty pounds of supplies, including a tent, a small cookstove, fuel bottle, and utensils. She rejected the idea of carrying a gun.

"There are people who want to rob someone or rape someone or mug someone," Jean says, "but I just decided somewhere along the way that those people were not going to climb a mountain to find a victim."

The hike was not considered lightly. The thought was intimidating, she says, but once on the Appalachian Trail she gained a fresh perspective. "It was such a metaphor for life's journey, you know? As you went along the trail sometimes you had to really remember to stop and see all the beauty that was along the way," says Jean. "It was like the old adage, 'It was the journey not the destination,' that was so true out there."

Jean Deeds reached the end at Mount Katahdin, Maine, on September 26, 1995. She had been on the trail a total of 175 days and nights.

 **RAY'S UPDATE: Jean's hike on the Appalachian Trail has produced hiking tours around the world, numerous speaking engagements, and a book, *There Are Mountains to Climb.***

The Tire Lady

Lorraine Waters   August 23, 1996

One at a time she bounced tires from a worn Ford van. One at a time, until Lorraine Waters had removed more than a hundred of them and stacked them in piles so passing motorists could see them.

It was a hot August day in 1996 when I met Lorraine doing what she had been doing every day to support her son and herself. This inspiration of a woman was selling tires rather than take a handout.

I asked how many tires she had. "Oh, my Lord," she says. "On a good day I'll handle anywheres from two to three hundred tires every day. There's over a hundred in the van. I load 'em and unload 'em every day."

Lorraine has been doing this since 1980; she started when she was only seventeen. "I started buying 'em for a dollar and two dollars apiece at that time," she says. "I'd clean 'em up and sell 'em for five or six dollars. That's how I originally got started doing it and then I got to liking it and I've been doing it ever since. There's been rough times that I really wanted to give up on it, you know? But, I stuck it out. Everybody said you can do it and I stuck with it and I'm proud of it."

Lorraine was also proud that she had raised her son on her own and trimmed her weight from three hundred pounds to one hundred thirty-five. She doesn't care if people say she's doing a man's work. "It probably is man's work," says Lorraine, "but I love doing it 'cause I'm just as good as a man if not better. I've been doing it for a long time. There's nothing I can't do with them, and when you see me dismount one by hand that's when you're going to be amazed."

And I was. Before long a fellow drove in and bought a used tire. Lorraine jacked up his car, dismounted his old tire, and mounted his new one all in the space of three minutes and forty seconds—flat!

Afterwards she tells me, "Like I say, I didn't want to get on welfare or food stamps, and I didn't want to ask nobody for help, and I figure if I could do it on my own, I'll do it. And for people to say they can't get a job, I don't believe that. There's jobs for everyone."

As I left she was changing another tire.

Dishwasher

Murray Wilson   October 1996

Murray Wilson is the dishwasher at a small restaurant in Winchester, Indiana.

The dishes go out with food on them and shortly thereafter they come back, dirty. How many dishes do you suppose Murray washes? "Quite a bit," he says. "It just varies a day 'cause I work like six days a week eight hours a day and sometimes it's real, real busy and sometimes you just never know."

You may notice that Murray has a slight limp. He needs ankle surgery but can't afford it right now. Nevertheless, he has walked for the March of Dimes, Diabetes, Cancer Society, Heart Association, and the United Way. He has raised more than fourteen thousand dollars.

"This is my fifth year," he says with a broad smile. "I started back in October of '91."

Ray: "How many miles do you suppose you've walked in that time?"

Murray: "I'd say close to fifty miles."

"And your feet hurt all the time?"

"Uh huh. Yes"

"So then why do you walk these walks?"

"I just want to walk and help people 'cause I care about it."

Because of his extraordinary efforts thirty-five-year-old Murray has been honored as a Distinguished Hoosier by Gov. Evan Bayh, and Second District Congressman Dave McIntosh rose on the floor of the House of Representatives to proclaim Murray Wilson a Hoosier Hero.

A dishwasher is seldom seen out front. But here's one fellow we thought everyone should know about. A guy with bad ankles and a sound heart.

 **RAY'S UPDATE: Although still bothered by bad ankles, Murray persists in walking for charity, helping to raise money for a variety of causes. As of 2003, he had raised more than $20,000. Murray, along with his wife and daughter, now live in Portland, Indiana.**

Brother Tom Elliott

A barking dog sends word that somebody's in the holler. We are in the hills of southeastern Kentucky, where strangers aren't always welcome, especially those with the prying eye of a camera. We have been warned the locals don't like to be held up for someone to gawk at and possibly ridicule.

But into the town of Hazard comes a mission from Indianapolis. It is the Mission on Wheels, the work of Brother Tom Elliott and his assistant John Turner. A truck loaded with at least five tons of food, clothing, and furniture backs up through a light fog and into a public picnic area at the edge of town.

Waiting in the gray morning chill is a representative of the Lively Stones Ministries of Hazard who says, "We invited a hundred families. That's 411 people, including 215 children and 196 adults."

The line is a long one. There are tired men in overalls, women in print dresses and worn coats, and children who hold back their smiles. Look past the faces of want and desperation to what you can't see: a shack, maybe with no indoor plumbing, no windows, perhaps dirt for a floor. As John Turner puts it, "This is not a Third World country here. This is the United States of America. But that's why we come back."

Tom Elliott has been coming to these hills once or twice a month since 1988. On this visit he was honored by a proclamation from Kentucky's governor, read aloud by the pastor of Hazard's Lively Stones Ministries, "Know ye that Thomas E. Elliott is hereby commissioned a Kentucky Colonel." There was more to the proclamation, and when it was finished everyone applauded.

So why, you might wonder, would these people travel all night long to help folks when there are plenty of Hoosiers who could use some assistance?

Tom's National Christian Outreach provides seventeen hundred meals a day in Indiana, four million in the past eight years. He comes here because the need is so acute, as one of those on line can attest: "Oh, it helps me a bunch. It helped me to get food for my little girls to have a nice Thanksgiving and stuff. I really appreciate it."

We stood off to the side, and I listened as Brother Tom explained: "Not until industry moves down here and starts putting some of these people to work is it going to remove the hunger and the suffering. Many of these families only eat one meal a day because they don't have anything else."

Tom Elliott was once a high roller, a drug and alcohol abuser until he learned something that most of us only think about over the holidays: the real fulfillment in life is giving. "You can't have the love of God in your heart and not share it with others," he says.

Within an hour and a half the truck was unloaded and its treasure taken back into the hills. There will be another twenty-hour round-trip by the Mission on Wheels next week.

 **RAY'S UPDATE: Tom assisted others until his death on November 22, 1998.**

Forgotten Hero

It's time to honor a policeman who fell in the line of duty. It happened in June 1922 when Indianapolis Police Department officer William Whitfield was shot in an alley near Thirty-sixth Street and College Avenue. He was a twelve-year police veteran, the fifteenth officer to die on duty, and the first African American. His assailant was white, and politics of the day meant there was minimal press coverage, a small article, and no photograph.

There is a picture, however, in the police wing of the City County Building, part of a display honoring IPD officers killed in the line of duty. Today, at Crown Hill Cemetery, there is another photo of Officer Whitfield, who until now had lain in an unmarked grave.

"I'm kind of an amateur historian," explains Detective Wayne Sharp. "I write articles for the IPD newsletter and it just so happened that the September issue carried my article about William Whitfield. There was a spontaneous uprising after that, and within a short time we had the money together and ordered a monument."

Assistant IPD Chief Robert Allen remembers, "My grandparents used to tell me a long time ago that a dead person could not rest in an unmarked grave. So, I'm saying surely and certainly with the honor that has been bestowed to Officer Whitfield that he is resting in peace today."

Officer Whitfield was divorced with no children, but there was family at the grave site, all wearing blue.

They snapped to attention and drew their hands quickly to the brim of their hats as rifles signaled a twenty-one gun salute. "Taps" was played from a nearby hilltop and an officer, killed in the line of duty seventy-six years ago, was honored for his sacrifice.

 **RAY'S UPDATE: The Indianapolis Police Department hopes to move Whitfield's grave to the police section at Crown Hill, but have not been able to find any living relatives to consent to the change.**

Friendship Spoons

Debbie Cunningham [Wofford]   January 1999

With a little practice and a piece of wood, you can make a lot of things. But what Debbie Cunningham [Wofford] is making you can't see unless you look closely.

The electric saw whines into your ears, dust floats into your hair and your eyes as Debbie takes the eight-inch pieces of wood to tables where anxious hands await. Debbie is helping these people make a life.

Each of the half dozen part-time employees is developmentally disabled. Each had difficulty keeping a job before coming to Debbie's art studio to make what are called Friendship Spoons.

"Back in the seventeenth century," Debbie says, "when sailors would go out to sea they would carve for their sweethearts spoons rather than give them rings. And the greater the carving, the greater the love."

Gaze around this workroom and you might wonder, "How great is the love here?" How great the love for a job and a measure of independence?

Jane is extremely nervous with a stranger and a camera but manages, haltingly, to note, "Right now I'm working on one of the four hearts and I'm working on the top part right now."

Johanna smiles broadly and proclaims, "I like it. Keeps me busy. I only work three days a week. The rest of the time I'm at home cleaning house."

Patty is proud of her accomplishments. "I carved two and turned around and sanded two," she says. "The same two I carve, I sand. And, you know, it took me the whole day to do both jobs. But that satisfied me."

For her efforts, Debbie receives no funding and no profits. "We struggle," she says. "We work on a shoestring. The sale of the spoons goes towards the building, the supplies, their wages."

Know anybody who complains about going to work? Anybody who doesn't like their job? Talk to Debbie. "These guys go through more stress and more fights just to live a normal life and they never give up," she notes. "It is incredible what I have learned from them."

Perhaps we can all learn from them. It's a message as timeless as the friendship spoon.

 **RAY'S UPDATE: Originals by D.E.B., 871 Conner Street, is located on the square in Noblesville.**

Terri Panszi

"Hi baby. She's so scared. Her name is Glory and she's the best cat. I mean she is the best."

Glory has just arrived at a place that will save her life and reacted as a cat will.

"Meow?!"

Glory is one lucky cat. Her owner can't keep her, but Glory will find a new home through the Animal Rescue Fund, ARF for short.

Since June 1998 ARF has found homes for more than six hundred animals, including drop-offs and those rescued from the streets.

ARF was founded by Terri Panszi, who explains what happens when someone wants to adopt a pet: "We do our homework. We have them fill out an adoption application. We ask for references, past history on pet ownership. Who their veterinarian is or was. And, we call."

If it weren't for ARF, most of the animals saved would have been euthanized. Put to sleep, forever.

"Not an option, is it sweetie?" Terri asks Glory. And she wonders how many didn't find refuge. "Oh, far too many. And spaying and neutering is the only answer. It truly is."

The number of unwanted dogs and cats killed each year in Indiana is staggering. At animal control facilities and humane societies the toll is in the thousands. By any measure it's a tragedy.

"I would really like to see all of the larger facilities implement a spay-neuter program before the animals ever leave the building," says Terri. "That's the only answer to the problem—reducing the population."

But, here there is refuge from the horror. "Hi sweeties. Hi sweeties."

Here somebody really cares.

 **RAY'S UPDATE: Since its inception, ARF has rescued approximately six thousand animals. The growing service has moved to a larger facility and has added another location called Kitty Corner. ARF relies on donations from the community and volunteer help to keep its doors open.**

Summer Place

Jim Richardson May 3, 1999

There's a song that goes back to the late 1950s called "A Summer Place." Tipton businessman Jim Richardson remembers the hit, and a while back he closed his eyes and thought about what such a place might be like.

"Well, it began as kind of a dream," he reveals, "fifteen or twenty years ago."

Today, not a hundred yards from Route 19 in Sharpsville, there it is. A little town called Summer Place. There's a Standard gas station, a barbershop, and a stainless-steel diner with all the equipment needed to fry burgers and make malts. All of it is right out of Jim's dream—a 1955 Ford, a '53 Mercury, and a '57 Chevy. And, in the fire station, a '55 Mack fire truck. There's also the marquee from the old Isis theater in Kokomo. Some of the old-timers called it the Is Is.

"We have a little bit of everything," says Jim. "We also have bicycles. About a hundred from the 30s, 40s, and 50s."

"How long did it take to put all of this together?" I ask.

"I've been doing this about four and a half years," Jim says.

"Four and a half years? You work pretty quickly, Jim, don't you?"

"Yea. Heh, heh, heh. Heh."

"This is fantastic!"

"Thank you, Ray. We've got a lot to do, yet. Everywhere I look I see work."

He also sees the 1950s as a positive, happy time.

"It's amazing," Jim reflects. "In America you can do anything you want to do if you're willing to work. And I think a lot of people are missing that today."

So, Jim Richardson has discovered what was always promised: America is where dreams come true. Like Summer Place.

RAY'S UPDATE: Jim and his wife Tricia have used Summer Place to help support children's charitable organizations, including the Riley Hospital for Children, Make a Wish Foundation, Saint Jude Hospital, and Easter Seals. Through their own nonprofit organization, A Home for Every Child, the Richardsons have helped fund the placement of nearly two hundred unwanted babies. What power there is in a dream.

Clowns

Don and Ruby Berkoski September 1999

How far would you go for a smile? I know a couple who travels thousands of miles a year to bring laughs to people in prisons, hospitals, and nursing homes.

Don Berkoski is a salesman who took up clowning as a way to give. His nickname became his clown name: Ski.

His wife Ruby is made up as a white-face clown. Her first time out she jokingly shouted a fanfare, "Ta Dah," which became her clown name.

The mid-afternoon sun drifts through the windows into the nursing home dining room, which doubles as a general activities center. There were about two dozen residents, some in wheelchairs, some seated at tables, chatting softly, others dozing on a recliner or sofa. Suddenly there was a burst of laughter from the hall and there, in the doorway, was Ski, a tramp clown in the Emmett Kelly tradition. As spotty applause awoke those asleep, Ski strode in acknowledging the welcome, his big clown shoes flopping merrily on the tile floor. "Well, hello. Thank you. Thank you," he says. His tattered pants, patched blue blazer, bright red nose, and crumpled hat said more than he did. A clown is always welcome.

Ta Dah was close behind, carrying a huge pink comb that she instantly put to use to the giggles of the lady she groomed in clown fashion. Ta Dah wore a bright blue outfit with a matching blue-sequined top hat.

As Ski and Ta Dah move about the room, you can see their routine is nothing extraordinary, really. It's what they do that is. It's what they give.

Ski encourages a lady who is thoroughly enjoying these whimsical visitors to tweak his red nose, which creates a loud whistle and, of course, a smile. "Look at that smile," Ski says. "What a smile."

Ruby acknowledges all of this didn't come easily for her. "I used to be very uncomfortable in nursing homes with people and now going in is just so different," she says. "They accept you without any reservations and you don't notice anything about them except they are people who need a hug or a smile. The rewards are a thousandfold. It's worth more than if I had earned a million dollars."

The Berkoskis are not paid for their appearances. They do it all for nothing. Or do they? As Ski points out, "The greatest pay that you'll ever receive as a human being is to do something for someone else."

 RAY'S UPDATE: Don passed away in 2001 at the age of sixty-two. Ruby, who now lives in Valparaiso, and her daughter have continued Smiles Unlimited, training with videos Don made before he died. They have 18 chapters and 400 dues-paying members in Indiana and Ohio.

Lucious Newsom

March 2000

Drive through a neighborhood where people don't have a lot and after a while you'll probably see Lucious Newsom. He drives a van with a sign on the side reading, "The Lord's Pantry."

"I think it's a shame to have a coat on and riding in a van," he says. "I'm warm and I'm passing a man on the street who is trembling from cold."

Lucious may be the most generous man you'll ever meet. His admirers will tell you he has donated ten years of his life to helping the needy. An outreach minister with Saint Luke Catholic Church, he goes out with his Lord's Pantry, rain or shine, pulls up to a street corner and gets out, letting people know he is here again.

He'll knock on a door and shout, "Food truck's out here."

And they come out, knowing they'll be able to get something to help them through another week. Soon appearing from the van are bags of canned goods, boxed food, and paper products—essential items free for the giving.

"Oh, he's wonderful," a resident tells me. "If it weren't for him, we'd all be in a fix sometimes. So, he's a good guy."

Reverend Newsom talks softly with someone in obvious distress. "Don't worry about the rent," Lucious tells him. "I'm going to pay it."

"Every day he comes through here. He's a blessing," someone tells me while walking past, arms clutching two sacks of groceries.

To another, Lucious gives a five-dollar bill and says, "Buy some bread."

Lucious says hunger takes no holiday, so neither does he.

"You do this seven days a week?" I ask.

"Yes sir. Starts at five thirty in the mornings."

"And you're all over town?"

"Yea."

I asked how he pays for it all? "I'm the Lord's biggest beggar," he answers. "I beg."

And what he gets he gives. "Indianapolis is a great town," says Lucious. "People in Indianapolis will give if they know you are going to do the right thing."

Lucious Newsom retired from pastoring in Chattanooga, Tennessee, when he was seventy, but was soon called again. Now eighty-one, you'll still find him out there in one neighborhood or another where some folks don't have it so good.

Vic Cook

April 2000

They say the best things in life are free. Thousands of kids a year learn about one of them tucked back in the woods of Pendleton, Indiana.

Crossing a fifteen-foot long hanging bridge, the visiting class climbs a stone path and goes through a simple enough doorway. Inside, they descend several steps to the sound of computer-generated music. They are inside a unique home built into a hillside.

A welcome is given by technical consultant Don Burrell: "All of the equipment here is being powered off of the twelve-volt batteries charged by solar energy." And he points to "the state of the art computer system where Vic works on video and also audio."

Living in perfect harmony with nature—cutting-edge technology and all—is the creation and inspiration of local professional musician Vic Cook, who calls it the Giant. He came up with the name by paraphrasing the proclamation of astronaut Neil Armstrong, the first man to walk on the moon. "This was a chance to make a giant leap for the environment if you will," says Vic. "And so the name for the house really came from that giant leap for mankind."

Virtually all of the energy is free—energy from the surrounding woodland, energy from the sun, and geothermal energy from the earth.

Vic leads his visitors to one of his innovations. "The refrigerator is from a hollowed beech log for the aesthetics," he says, "and then inside is a really hi-tech, solar-powered refrigeration unit."

Completed in 1978, the Giant remains as one of man's dramatic philosophical statements on the environment and society.

"Every one of us has a unique talent," Vic reflects. "And unfortunately, in my opinion, most of our lives are stolen away by the high cost of living. So, this is really a study in being close to nature and being able to do it for free."

After an hour's tour of the Giant, Vic leads his visitors back across the footbridge. A teacher never knows the reach of his influence. Every year thousands of young visitors get a different view of things here, a different dream. Vic Cook's dream is to make a difference.

 **RAY'S UPDATE: Schools from around the state continue to bring students on day trips to see the Giant in the woods.**

Tony Stewart

Since he was eight years old, Tony Stewart has been going around a track somewhere trying to be first. But NASCAR's rookie of the year for 1999 has discovered what a busy career he has chosen.

"Everything that I thought would be glamorous about this sport has been that and tenfold," he tells me. "But there's a lot of pressures, a lot of stresses and strains, and obligations and things that you have to do that you don't think about."

There are personal appearances, constant travel, and one thing he learned early: the importance of merchandising.

"If you went to the racetrack and you blew a motor in hot laps you didn't get paid," notes Tony. "And just because you didn't get paid at the racetrack doesn't mean the grocery bill didn't exist and didn't mean the rent didn't exist anymore. So, you sold your t-shirts out of your car after the race was over to help with the income."

Today, Tony sells hundreds of things that bear his name, including t-shirts, hats, jackets, even flashlights. If you aren't able to visit his little store, there is a catalog and now a web site.

But none of it would happen without the race. And he says he learned it all as he went along.

"I think racing has taught me lessons about life, too," he reflects. "I mean, it's just learning experiences. And every day you learn about something that's going to help you tomorrow and it's not only that way in racing. It's that way in life."

Tony Stewart earns more from his off-track business than he does behind the wheel. But in the cockpit is where he'd rather be any day.

RAY'S UPDATE: True Speed Enterprises, Inc., is a corporation owned by Tony, 2002 NASCAR Winston Cup Champion. Tony also owns Tony Stewart Racing, Inc., which is the merchandise retail side of True Speed Enterprises. True Speed Enterprises, Inc., has many corporations under its umbrella. These corporations encompass Tony's many diversified interests. Most unique is the fact that Tony's family helps coordinate and manage all of these corporations. Tony's success in NASCAR's Winston Cup racing series has also greatly increased his success with True Speed Enterprises, Inc. You can visit Tony's web site at http://www.tonystewart.com.

Christmas-Basket Baby

Bob Denny December 2000

This story has some earmarks of a favorite Christmas movie, *It's a Wonderful Life*, starring Jimmy Stewart. You know the one. A sort of "What if?" What if George Bailey had never been born? In this case it's what if Bob Denny had never been found.

But he was.

It was snowing on Christmas Eve 1919 when a baby was left in a basket at an interurban railway station in Hancock County. The snow was four inches deep.

"There was a little hole and some kids were playing and they thought they heard some kittens and so they went over there scraped it off and it was a baby, crying," says Bob Denny, who has told his story many times in the eight decades since he was found. "They took me over to a doctor and he said I had to have breast milk or I was going to die."

The story goes they found only one woman willing to help.

"She nursed me for two weeks and that happened to be a black lady," says Bob. "There wasn't no white woman willing to share. But she did and she said, 'Now, you bring me that baby!'"

A newspaper report of the "Baby in the Basket" goes on to explain that the infant was named Bob Denny. And, he grew up and went to war.

"I was all over England," notes Bob, tracing his travels on a sixty-year-old map of Europe. "I crossed over here from Portsmouth, England, to Cherbourg . . . and on to Utah Beach."

A magazine photo on D-Day shows Private Robert Denny aboard ship, heading for Normandy and the battle ahead.

Time-aged discharge papers tell what happened after that, where he served and the medals he earned. He fought in the Battle of the Bulge and earned five Bronze Stars. Later in Germany, Corporal Denny killed a Nazi SS officer and took his armband. He still has it.

"I got four years in the military combat zone and lost a couple of buddies with me and I came home without anything," says Bob. "So the good Lord's watching out for me, I reckon."

The good Lord has been watching over Bob Denny ever since two children heard an infant whimpering in the snow.

"I'll tell you one thing," he says. "It's better than being put into a black bag and thrown into a trash can. I've thought about that a lot of times."

After the war Bob married, had three children and four grandchildren, and drove a truck for twenty-five years. He's eighty-one now, a widower with a remarkable story of how a life began in 1919 on Christmas Eve.

 RAY'S UPDATE: Bob says he never learned the identity of his natural parents. His stepfather offered the only clue. In the basket with him they found a white handkerchief with a monogrammed letter "S." Nothing else.

Good Samaritan Clinic

Becky Evans   June 2001

Meet Becky Evans, the woman who launched a clinic. It took twenty years for the Good Samaritan Clinic to happen and, as Becky explains, it was not by intention. "I just went over to the Mission and started doing blood pressures and wound dressings as I saw the need. I did not work here. I had another job. I was the nurse at the federal building," she says.

That was in 1981 when Becky's husband was director of the Good News Ministries on East Washington Street. A clinic was formally established in 1993 and has since moved into a new building thanks to foundation grants, contributions, and individual effort. "We've had so much volunteer help," notes Becky. "One caulking company came and did all the caulking. A wallpaper company donated all the wallpaper and put it up. And then there's the floor and the baseboard. I mean it's just been one donation after another. And brick by brick it was just put together." The one-story building has a reception desk and waiting area, several examining rooms, and a dispensary that offers nonprescription medication for minor ailments.

In the year 2000 there were more than four thousand patient visits attended by a volunteer staff of doctors and nurses, and now the clinic is open to anyone who needs medical help.

"I hope that the work we do there will be pleasing," Becky says. "We look forward to helping a lot of people in the community, there's a great need there."

RAY'S UPDATE: By the end of 2002 Becky had counted more than thirty-six hundred visits to the clinic, offering basic nonprescription foot, dental, and pediatric care and cancer screening in addition to general medical counseling. The Sycamore Foundation recognized Becky's vision and dedication by giving her the prestigious Indiana Achievement Award. The clinic is located at 11 Eastern Avenue in Indianapolis.

City Garden

August 2001

Gardening is not one of those things you would expect a city kid to learn, but here they are, smack dab in the middle of Indianapolis growing tomatoes, beans, and cabbages. And their teachers are some students from Brebeuf Jesuit Preparatory School.

Team leader Samantha Hurst puts it this way: "I guess we were just fed up with the system at school and the community service part of it and we wanted to kind of step outside our north side community so we came down here, found an empty lot, and put in the garden, and it's been going great ever since."

The garden in the city is growing on a vacant lot on College Avenue just north of Seventeenth Street. About two dozen youngsters from age six to sixteen digging in the dirt, weeding, mulching, and watering, and now in late summer they get to take home some fresh vegetables.

"This lot is my grandfather's," says fellow student Michael Star. "He had owned an apartment on it. They tore it down about twenty or twenty-five years ago and he'd been just cutting the grass. Sam and I had this idea about the garden and he said, 'I've got a lot and you guys can go garden.'"

It started in the spring with neighborhood kids from the nearby Citizens Multi-Service Center. Samantha describes the program as, "Really neat and we hope to expand it next year and there are a couple of IPS schools who have contacted us to see if we want to do a garden for them. So this was just sort of trial and error. We're just a bunch of kids coming out to have a good time, do something new. And it's been a new experience. Step outside the box."

Step outside the box and you might just grow something else in the garden.

 RAY'S UPDATE: Samantha is today majoring in art at the University of San Diego. She continues to volunteer her skills, serving in such countries as Mexico and the Dominican Republic. Michael is currently a student at the Massachusetts Institute of Technology, where he plans on majoring in engineering.

Gus Streeter

Gus Streeter was born on September 29, 1896, and in the one hundred five years since he has seen it all. From the horse and buggy and kerosene lamps to automobiles, manned flight, the telephone, radio, television, space exploration, and much more. One memory, however, outweighs all the others.

"Well," he says, "I can't forget going into the service and seeing what war is like. War is hell on earth."

Gus went to fight in France, was wounded twice as he single-handedly destroyed an enemy communications network, and was presented France's highest military decoration, the Croix de Guerre.

But there was another honor denied him until now because his wounds had not been documented: the Purple Heart.

"You know, that Purple Heart has a good meaning to me," Gus says. "It shows me, as France did, that they cared for me and my deeds. Now, as I get this Purple Heart, it shows me and France that America also cares for me."

Gus was determined to wait for the medal he earned in combat so long, long ago. And, so it was that eighty-three years after it all happened, he learned that America indeed cares. On November 8, 2001, Gus was awarded the Purple Heart in a special ceremony at the Indiana War Memorial in Indianapolis.

RAY'S UPDATE: Gus passed away quietly in his sleep barely a week after the long-delayed honor was bestowed.

Gus lived his closing years at the Saint Augustine Home in Indianapolis, where his caregivers said to his final days he had an occasional Rob Roy cocktail and smoked four cigars daily.

Richard Vine

December 2001

Born in the wine-growing region of upper New York State, today's "Indiana's Own" is now the Wine Consultant for American Airlines. He is also a professor of enology, the science of wines, at Purdue University.

Some of the tools may be different today, but wine has been made essentially the same way for thousands of years. Fruit juice ferments, sugar turns to alcohol, and "Voila!"

Professor Richard Vine (no, we're not making that up) has been researching wine for the past forty years, twelve of those years at Purdue.

"Well, one of the things we have learned that is perhaps more important than others," he explains professorially, "is the art of filtration. And, we have learned how to keep wine longer, how to improve the quality from grapes that come in thousands of varieties."

Wine making, once considered magic, is today a science. What has not changed are the basic chemical and biological reactions that occur in the fermentation process.

Richard continues, "Alcohol is produced by yeast cells creating enzymes, which transform six carbon sugars into ethyl alcohol and a little bit of heat energy and carbon dioxide gas. When carbon dioxide is no longer produced, the fermentation is finished and the wine is made."

Since he makes wine, I asked if he also drinks it.

"Absolutely! My wife and I generally have a glass or two a day with dinner," he says, "which is highly recommended by most of the medical community nowadays. A couple of glasses of red wine are thought to be good for you."

"And you believe that then?"

"Absolutely. Absolutely, yes. I feel I'm as healthy as most sixty-three year olds, and I've drunk wine for forty years."

Now, don't get the wrong idea. The enology lab makes about three thousand gallons of wine a year. What is not used for research is washed down the drain.

RAY'S UPDATE: Retired from Purdue University since 2000, Professor Vine continues to teach a popular wine appreciation course in West Lafayette. He also maintains his Purdue duties assisting new and developing wineries around the state and chairs the Indy International Wine Competition, which has become one of the largest wine judgings in the country.

Matt O'Neil

January 26, 2002

A coffeehouse in a campus town is about as common as fish in a stream. Although at this coffeehouse the fish are in a bathtub.

You'll find them at the Runcible Spoon in Bloomington. The Spoon has been there for years and so have the fish. As Matt O'Neal, the owner, explains, "A waitress left on vacation a while back and put the fish in the bathtub until she returned. Trouble is she never came back." That was in 1978, and since that time customers and staff have cared for the fish. In case you're wondering, the tub was left in place when the structure was converted to a coffeehouse.

Through the years, new fish replaced those who swam on to fish heaven, and they have always received the best food, clean water, plants and rocks, and murals on the wall. There were three fish in the first place. And there are still three fish—goldfish.

The Runcible Spoon is now mixing longtime clientele with new customers since Matt took over. Matt is a master chef formerly with La Tour restaurant, the Columbia Club, and the Crystal Room in Indianapolis, and the proprietor of the Walden Inn in Greencastle. Today, he blends gourmet cuisine with the atmosphere of a coffeehouse.

 RAY'S UPDATE: Runcible Spoon is taken from the fairy tale "The Owl and the Pussycat." *The American Heritage Dictionary* defines runcible spoon as a three-pronged fork, such as a pickle fork, curved like a spoon and having a cutting edge.

A Brief History

WISH-TV, Channel 8 signed on the air in Indianapolis on July 1, 1954, almost thirteen years after the initial broadcast of WISH Radio. On the initial broadcast, a fifteen-minute program introduced the station's approximately sixty-five staff members and eleven local owners. The staff now numbers more than one hundred and fifty people working in news, sales, programming, creative services, production, engineering, traffic, and accounting. For the first year WISH-TV broadcast from one of the WISH radio towers until a one thousand-foot tower was built and the station was able to increase its coverage. The current tower that is used was built in 1995. The station moved to its current location on Meridian Street in 1965.

Among some of the early broadcasters were Vince Leonard, a former WISH radio personality who is remembered as the first WISH-TV news anchor, and Stan Wood, who joined the staff in the late 1960s.

Current news director Lee Giles began working at WISH-TV in 1963, while Mike Ahern joined the staff in 1967. Debby Knox joined the news team in 1980.

Today the station serves more than 3.2 million viewers and is best known locally for its commitment to twenty-four-hour news.

2004 marks the station's fiftieth anniversary, and viewers can be sure that they will continue to get the very best from WISH-TV for many years to come.